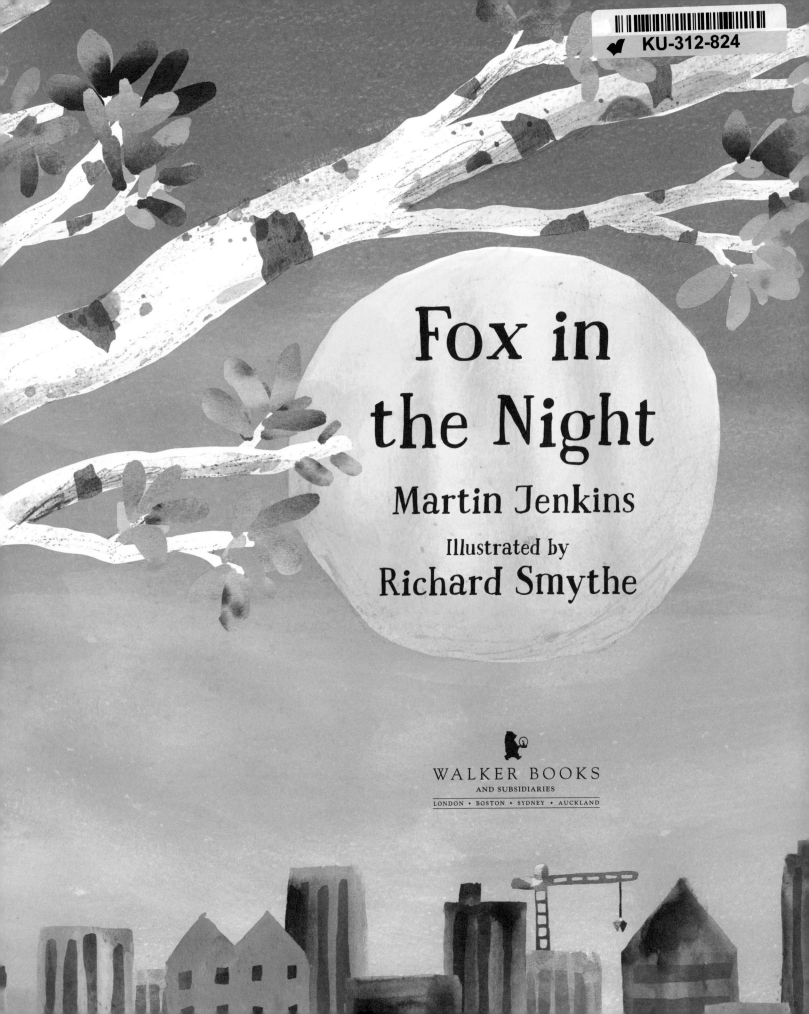

Fox in the Night

Martin Jenkins

Illustrated by
Richard Smythe

WALKER BOOKS
AND SUBSIDIARIES
LONDON · BOSTON · SYDNEY · AUCKLAND

This is a book about
light and dark.

For Fern – R. S.

For Thomasina and Willow – M. J.

First published 2017 by Walker Books Ltd, 87 Vauxhall Walk, London SE11 5HJ

2 4 6 8 10 9 7 5 3 1

Text © 2017 Martin Jenkins   Illustrations © 2017 Richard Smythe

The right of Martin Jenkins and Richard Smythe to be identified as author and illustrator respectively of this work
has been asserted by them in accordance with the Copyrights, Designs and Patents Act 1988.

This book has been typeset in Kreon   Printed in China

British Library Cataloguing in Publication Data: a catalogue record
for this book is available from the British Library.

ISBN 978-1-4063-5515-4

www.walker.co.uk

Fox wakes up in her cosy den.
She's hungry!

It's dark in Fox's den because the daylight doesn't reach inside.

She walks to the entrance and looks outside.

The sun is shining brightly.

There are people about.

Perhaps she'd better wait a while.

She turns round and goes back to sleep.

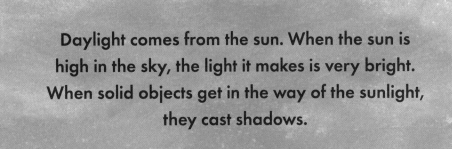

Daylight comes from the sun. When the sun is high in the sky, the light it makes is very bright. When solid objects get in the way of the sunlight, they cast shadows.

Fox wakes up again. She's even hungrier now.
The sun is going down and the people have all gone.
She leaves her den.

When the sun is lower in the sky, its light is less bright.
Shadows are longer too.

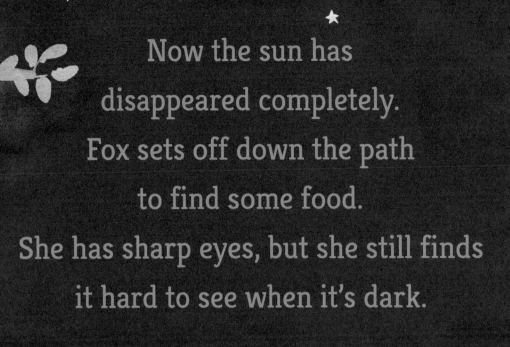

Now the sun has
disappeared completely.
Fox sets off down the path
to find some food.
She has sharp eyes, but she still finds
it hard to see when it's dark.

We need light to see things.
Even at night there is usually some light.

13

Moonlight is light from the sun that has bounced off the moon. Moonlight is much less bright than sunlight.

The moon has come out from behind a cloud. That's better. And there's more light ahead. Fox creeps forward. What's that?

The light shining on the mouse
comes from a streetlamp and is
made by electricity.

A mouse!

But the mouse is
too fast for Fox.

The mouse and Fox both cast shadows in the light from the streetlamp.

Fox is getting really hungry now.

Perhaps she'll find something tasty in a dustbin,
or a pizza that someone couldn't finish.

Suddenly she stops. She stares.

Another fox. She steps forwards.

The other fox steps towards her...

Light from the streetlamp bounces off the mirror in the shop
window and makes a reflection of Fox.

She steps forwards again.

Bump!

Fox can't see the glass that the window is made of,
because it's transparent and lets all the light through.

Something's coming.
Fox better get out of here.

That was close.

Parp! Parp!

Car headlights also use electricity to make light.

Fox turns down an alley.
Something smells interesting.

She slips through a hole in a fence.
She inches forward.
It's hot!

Very hot things often give off light.

But what's this?

Delicious!

Torches make light using electricity stored in batteries.

Time to go.

She's got her supper.
And there in the moonlight is the path
through the trees, leading her safely home.

THINKING ABOUT
LIGHT AND DARK

Stand outside in the sunlight.
How long is your shadow?
Stand outside again a couple of hours later.
Is your shadow longer or shorter?
Can you work out why?

INDEX

Look up the pages to find out more about light and dark.
Don't forget to look up both kinds of word, this kind – and this kind.

BIBLIOGRAPHY

Here are some other books about light and dark and science.

Oscar and the Moth by Geoff Waring,
Walker Books (2008)

Look Inside Science by Minna Lacey and Stefano Tognetti,
Usborne Books (2012)

First Encyclopedia of Science by Rachel Firth,
Usborne Books (2011)